D0759019

The Nile River

Claire Throp

Raintree

Chicago, Illinois

www.capstonepub.com
Visit our website to find out
more information about
Heinemann-Raintree books.

To order:
☎ Phone 800-747-4992
🖥 Visit www.capstonepub.com
to browse our catalog and order online.

Edited by Rebecca Rissman, Dan Nunn, and
    Catherine Veitch
Designed by Cynthia Della-Rovere
Leveling by Jeanne Clidas
Picture research by Elizabeth Alexander
Production by Victoria Fitzgerald
Originated by Capstone Global Library
Printed and bound in North Mankato, MN.
012013   007114RP

16 15 14 13
10 9 8 7 6 5 4 3 2

**Library of Congress Cataloging-in-
Publication Data**

Throp, Claire.
  The Nile River / Claire Throp.
    p. cm.—(Explorer tales)
  Includes bibliographical references and index.
  ISBN 978-1-4109-4784-0 (hb)—ISBN 978-1-
4109-4791-8 (pb) 1. Nile River—Discovery and
exploration—Juvenile literature. 2. Explorers—Af-
rica, Sub-Saharan—History—Juvenile literature. I.
Title. II. Series: Explorer tales.
  DT117.T47 2013
  916.204—dc23   2011041541

Acknowledgments
We would like to thank the following for permission
to reproduce photographs: Alamy pp. 8 (© John
Warburton-Lee Photography), 11 (© Gallo Images),
14-15 (© Juan Carlos Longos), 15 (© INTERFOTO),
17 (© Mary Evans Picture Library), 20 (© Eric Nathan),
27 (© Greenshoots Communications); Corbis pp. 18, 22
(© Hulton-Deutsch Collection); Getty Image10 (Hulton
Archive), 13 (Imagno/Hulton Archive), 16 (Eliot Elisofon/
Time Life Pictures), 19 (Hulton Archive); NASA p. 4;
Photolibrary pp. 9 (Leemage Leemage/Universal Images
Group), 23 (The British Library), 26 (William Gray/OSF);
Reuters p. 25 (Arthur Asiimwe); p. 24 © Scott Nydam;
Shutterstock pp. 6 (© Zeljko Radojko), 7 (© Francisco
Caravana), 12 (© Pasi Koskela), 21 (© Oleg Znamenskiy).

Cover photographs of Florence Baker reproduced
with permission of Getty Images (Hulton Archive);
birdseye view of Cairo, 1882, reproduced with
permission of Sanders of Oxford, rare prints & maps
(www.sandersofoxford.com); Murchison Falls, Uganda,
reproduced with permission of Shutterstock (© Oleg
Znamenskiy). Background image of Murchison Falls,
Uganda, reproduced with permission of Shutterstock
(© Oleg Znamenskiy).

Every effort has been made to contact copyright
holders of material reproduced in this book. Any
omissions will be rectified in subsequent printings
if notice is given to the publisher.

Disclaimer
All the Internet addresses (URLs) given in this book were
valid at the time of going to press. However, due to the
dynamic nature of the Internet, some addresses may
have changed, or sites may have changed or ceased to
exist since publication. While the author and publisher
regret any inconvenience this may cause readers, no
responsibility for any such changes can be accepted by
either the author or the publisher.

Contents

River of Mystery .4

The Source of the Nile 8

Early Explorers 10

Female Traveler 12

Arguing over Lake Victoria 14

Another Nile Source 18

Lost and Found 22

The Real Source? 24

Around the Nile Today 26

Timeline *28*

Explorer's Checklist *29*

Glossary *30*

Find Out More *31*

Index *32*

Some words are shown in bold, **like this**. You can find out what they mean by looking in the glossary.

River of Mystery

The Nile River is the longest river in the world, at 4,132 miles long. It travels through ten African countries. It is made up of two main rivers—the White Nile and the Blue Nile.

The Nile Delta is where the Nile River spreads out and goes into the sea.

Nile Delta

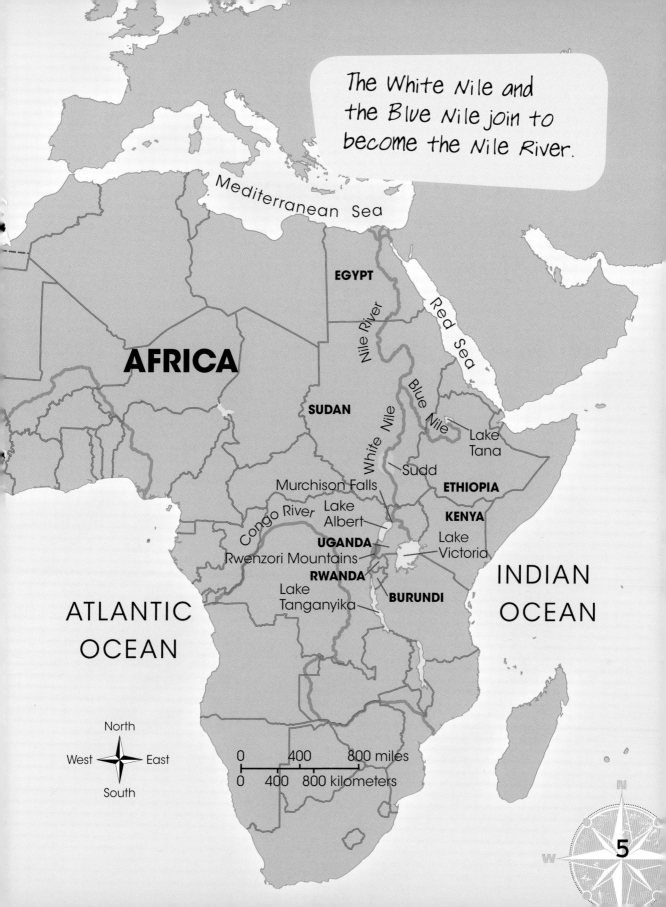

The White Nile and the Blue Nile join to become the Nile River.

Mediterranean Sea

EGYPT

Red Sea

Nile River

AFRICA

SUDAN

Blue Nile

White Nile

Lake Tana

Sudd

Murchison Falls

ETHIOPIA

Congo River

Lake Albert

KENYA

UGANDA

Lake Victoria

Rwenzori Mountains

RWANDA

Lake Tanganyika

BURUNDI

ATLANTIC OCEAN

INDIAN OCEAN

North
West — East
South

0   400   800 miles
0   400   800 kilometers

5

The Nile River floods every year. The floods make the land nearby very good for growing **crops**. The ancient Egyptians built their homes along the Nile River, near their crops.

The ancient Egyptians grew wheat to make bread.

Felucca boats sail on the Nile River.

The Source of the Nile

Where a river begins is known as the river's **source**. At one time, it was thought that the Nile River started in the snow-capped Rwenzori Mountains, in Uganda.

Rwenzori Mountains

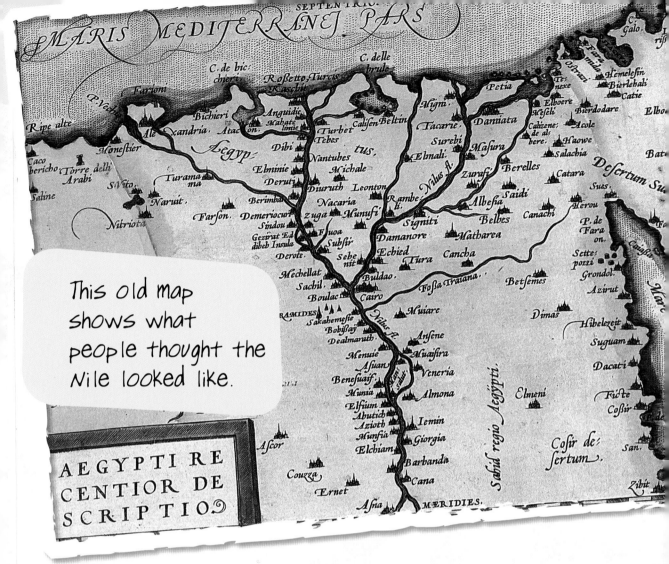

This old map shows what people thought the Nile looked like.

For thousands of years, there have been **expeditions** to find the source of the Nile. Many failed because of injuries, illness, and even death. The landscape was difficult to travel through, too.

Early Explorers

The Roman Emperor Nero sent soldiers to find the **source** of the Nile. They had to turn back because they could not travel through a **marshland** area called the **Sudd**. Plants grew so close together that the boats could not pass.

In 1770, James Bruce found the source of the Blue Nile in Ethiopia.

"Sudd" means "barrier" in Arabic. The Sudd, in Sudan, was certainly a barrier to explorers!

11

Female Traveler

In the early 1860s, Alexandrine-Pieternella-Françoise Tinné explored the White Nile in Sudan with her mother and aunt. At the time, women did not travel much—and certainly not on their own!

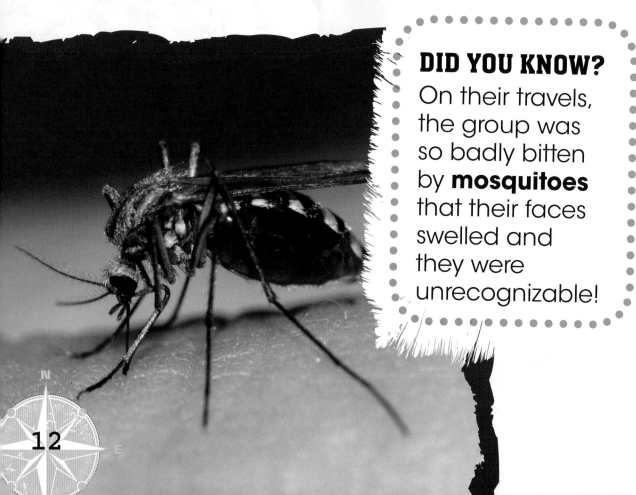

DID YOU KNOW?
On their travels, the group was so badly bitten by **mosquitoes** that their faces swelled and they were unrecognizable!

Alexandrine Tinné

Arguing over Lake Victoria

In 1857, John Hanning Speke and Richard Burton set out to find the **source** of the White Nile. Along the way, Burton became sick. Speke continued alone, and he reached Lake Victoria.

In 1858, Speke became the first European to see Lake Victoria, in Uganda.

Speke

Speke guessed that Lake Victoria was a source of the Nile. Burton did not believe him, and the men had a falling out over this.

A stone was laid to mark Speke's discovery of this source of the Nile River.

In 1862, John Hanning Speke discovered Ripon Falls on the coast of Lake Victoria. The water that flowed over these falls led to the White Nile. This was proof that Lake Victoria was the **source** of the Nile!

In 1860, Speke traveled to Africa again, this time with James Grant (on the left).

Another Nile Source

British explorer Samuel White Baker explored the White Nile from 1861 to 1862. On his journey, he met some interesting people. The people Baker met used cows' urine and ash to color their hair red!

Samuel White Baker

DID YOU KNOW?
Florence spoke many languages, rode camels and horses, and even carried a gun!

Samuel Baker's wife, Florence, traveled everywhere with him. It is thought she was once a **slave**, and that Baker met her while traveling in Europe.

In 1864, Baker found another lake and named it Lake Albert. Lake Albert gets water from the Victoria Nile, near Murchison Falls.

This village is on the shores of Lake Albert.

Lost and Found

David Livingstone set out to look for the Nile's **source** in 1866. He became extremely sick and lost touch with everyone he knew back in Great Britain. Many people thought he was dead.

An American man, Henry Stanley, was sent to find Livingstone. He found him in Tanzania. Livingstone was the only European there. Stanley asked a strange question: "Doctor Livingstone, I presume?" Later, Livingstone died before reaching the Nile's source.

The Real Source?

In 2006, explorers found what they think is the farthest **source** of the Nile River, in Nyungwe Forest in Rwanda. During their journey, they wrecked a raft and a plane. One explorer broke his leg, and the group was attacked by local rebels.

The source is known as the "Mac source." This is because all three men who discovered it have last names that start with "Mac"!

Around the Nile Today

In 2006, oil was discovered under Lake Albert. A pipeline to move the oil needs to be built. It will have to go through swamps and mountains, and it will cost a lot of money.

The discovery of oil has caused arguments over where people can fish.

People drill
for oil at
Lake Albert.

27

Timeline

66 CE Emperor Nero sends soldiers to find the **source** of the Nile.

1770 James Bruce announces he is the first European to reach the source of the Blue Nile.

1858 John Hanning Speke finds the source of the White Nile and calls it Lake Victoria.

1860s Alexandrine-Pieternella-Françoise Tinné explores the White Nile.

1861–1864 The Bakers explore the Nile and discover Lake Albert.

1871 Henry Stanley "finds" Livingstone.

2006 The "Ascend the Nile" explorers find what they think is the farthest source of the Nile.

Explorer's Checklist

If you want to go exploring, there are a few things you will need to take with you:

- ⦿ map and compass
- ⦿ food and water
- ⦿ sunblock
- ⦿ phone
- ⦿ hat
- ⦿ cool clothing
- ⦿ first-aid kit, including anti-**malaria** medicine
- ⦿ **mosquito** net to keep away the mosquitoes

Glossary

barrier something that blocks the way

crops plants that are grown for food—
for example, wheat

expedition journey to explore a particular area

malaria serious disease that humans get after
being bitten by a particular type of mosquito

marshland land that is often flooded with water
and difficult to travel through

mosquito biting insect that sucks blood and
spreads disease

slave person who is not paid for the work he or
she does

source place from which a river begins. Rivers
usually begin on high ground.

Sudd swampy area with thick plants near the
Nile River

Find Out More

Books

Adams, Simon. *Children's Great Explorers Encyclopedia.* New York: Parragon, 2008.

Bowden, Rob. *Settlements of the Nile River* (Rivers Through Time). Chicago: Heinemann Library, 2005.

Heinrichs, Ann. *The Nile* (Nature's Wonders). Tarrytown, N.Y.: Marshall Cavendish, 2008.

Websites

history.howstuffworks.com/african-history/nile-river.htm

Find out more about the Nile River on this website.

idahoptv.org/dialogue4kids/season11/rivers/facts.cfm

Learn more about rivers on this website.

Index

Baker, Florence 19
Baker, Samuel White
  18, 19, 20
Blue Nile 4, 5, 10
Bruce, James 10
Burton, Richard 14, 15

crops 6

Egyptians, ancient 6
Ethiopia 10
explorer's equipment
  29

felucca boats 7
floods 6

Lake Albert 20, 26–27
Lake Victoria 14–15,
  16
Livingstone, David
  22–23

maps 5, 9
Murchison Falls 20, 21

Nero, Emperor 10
Nile Delta 4

oil drilling 26–27

Ripon Falls 16
Rwanda 24

source of the Nile 8,
  9, 10, 14–16, 22, 23,
  24–25
Speke, John Hanning
  14–17
Stanley, Henry 23
Sudd 10, 11

Tinné, Alexandrine
  12–13

Uganda 8, 14

White Nile 4, 5, 12,
  16, 18